Celebrating the City of Cancun

Walter the Educator

Silent King Books

SILENT KING BOOKS

SKB

Copyright © 2024 by Walter the Educator

All rights reserved. No part of this book may be reproduced in any manner whatsoever without written permission except in the case of brief quotations embodied in critical articles and reviews.

First Printing, 2024

Disclaimer
This book is a literary work; the story is not about specific persons, locations, situations, and/or circumstances unless mentioned in a historical context. Any resemblance to real persons, locations, situations, and/or circumstances is coincidental. This book is for entertainment and informational purposes only. The author and publisher offer this information without warranties expressed or implied. No matter the grounds, neither the author nor the publisher will be accountable for any losses, injuries, or other damages caused by the reader's use of this book. The use of this book acknowledges an understanding and acceptance of this disclaimer.

Celebrating the City of Cancun is a collectible souvenir book that belongs to the Celebrating Cities Book Series by Walter the Educator. Collect them all and more books at WaltertheEducator.com

CANCUN

Beneath the azure veil of sky, Cancún lies,

Celebrating the City of
Cancun

A city where the sun's golden fingers softly caress

Celebrating the City of
Cancun

The turquoise cradle of the Caribbean's sighs,

Celebrating the City of Cancun

Where ancient whispers of Mayan gods bless.

Celebrating the City of Cancun

Oh Cancún, jewel of Quintana Roo's embrace,

Celebrating the City of
Cancun

Where the dawn unfurls with vibrant hues,

Celebrating the City of Cancun

In this paradise, every morn's a delicate lace,

Celebrating the City of Cancun

Of coral dawns and cerulean blues.

Celebrating the City of
Cancun

The ocean's breath, a rhythm of tranquil peace,

Celebrating the City of Cancun

With waves that dance upon the shore,

Celebrating the City of Cancun

In your embrace, all worries cease,

Celebrating the City of
Cancun

For your beauty's song, we all adore.

Celebrating the City of
Cancun

White sands, like powdered sugar, fine and pure,

Celebrating the City of
Cancun

Stretch out like dreams beneath the feet,

Celebrating the City of Cancun

A sanctuary where hearts find cure,

Celebrating the City of Cancun

And spirits, with the tides, compete.

Celebrating the City of
Cancun

In twilight's glow, your skyline alights,

Celebrating the City of
Cancun

With colors that paint the evening air,

Celebrating the City of
Cancun

Stars above and city lights,

Celebrating the City of Cancun

Reflecting on the waters, a pair so fair.

Celebrating the City of Cancun

Cancún, your nightlife's a carnival of delight,

Celebrating the City of
Cancun

From pulsating beats to gentle serenades,

Celebrating the City of Cancun

Underneath the moon's soft light,

Celebrating the City of Cancun

A symphony of laughter never fades.

Celebrating the City of
Cancun

The cenotes, crystal eyes of the earth,

Celebrating the City of
Cancun

Hold secrets in their liquid depths,

Celebrating the City of
Cancun

A testament to the land's rebirth,

Celebrating the City of Cancun

And nature's ancient, gentle breaths.

Celebrating the City of Cancun

Palms sway like dancers in the breeze,

Celebrating the City of
Cancun

Casting shadows, long and lean,

Celebrating the City of Cancun

Their rustling leaves whisper to the seas,

Celebrating the City of Cancun

In a language only nature can convene.

Celebrating the City of Cancun

The markets buzz with vibrant life,

Celebrating the City of Cancun

Stalls adorned with crafts and fare,

Celebrating the City of Cancun

Every corner a blend of culture rife,

Celebrating the City of
Cancun

A tapestry woven with intricate care.

Celebrating the City of Cancun

Through streets where history meets today,

Celebrating the City of
Cancun

Murals tell stories of times long past,

Celebrating the City of
Cancun

The Mayan legacy, here to stay,

Celebrating the City of Cancun

In every stone, forever cast.

Celebrating the City of Cancun

ABOUT THE CREATOR

Walter the Educator is one of the pseudonyms for Walter Anderson. Formally educated in Chemistry, Business, and Education, he is an educator, an author, a diverse entrepreneur, and he is the son of a disabled war veteran. "Walter the Educator" shares his time between educating and creating. He holds interests and owns several creative projects that entertain, enlighten, enhance, and educate, hoping to inspire and motivate you.

Follow, find new works, and stay up to date
with Walter the Educator™
at WaltertheEducator.com